The Surname Kellogg

Susan Morris &
Wendy Bosberry-Scott

ISBN: 1540498700
ISBN-13: 978-1540498700

The question of surnames, their origins, distribution and history, lies at the heart of genealogy as well as being fascinating in its own right.

In the 1980s and 1990s, long before many genealogical sources were even indexed, let alone online, our Surname Report service provided expert assessments of the origins, history and distribution of selected British surnames, using the sources available at the time.

Now, with so many more sources available, we believe that these reports retain their value as studies of individual surnames, and so we are gradually making the Debrett Surname Archive available online and in print for the first time. Some modern indexes have been consulted to refresh and update the reports.

Debrett Ancestry Research Ltd, PO Box 379,
Winchester SO23 9YQ
Tel: 01962 841904
Email: info@debrettancestry.co.uk
Website: www.debrettancestry.co.uk

CONTENTS

1   Overview   1

2   Origins and Early Examples   3

3   Distribution   6

4   Printed Genealogies   13

5   Summary   14

6   Sources Consulted   16

Overview

The use of surnames in England began in the Norman period, when surnames were not necessarily hereditary but usually a form of description. Some described the individual's trade or profession; others were nicknames; some gave the father's Christian name; others gave the individual's place of residence or origin.

Different surnames might be used in different documents, or more than one surname given in one document. Early descriptions were fairly elaborate and by the thirteenth and fourteenth centuries these were simpler, but still variable, and indeed the instability of surnames continued until well into the seventeenth century.

Although some Normans would already have had hereditary surnames on their arrival in Britain, the passing on of a surname from generation to generation only became customary in Britain gradually during the course of the thirteenth and fourteenth centuries. At the end of this period most of the population apparently had surnames.

Variations in the spelling of a family's surname continue to be found until the present century. Before this, as most people could not read or write, the parish clerk or other official would write down the name as they heard it.

There are four main groups of surnames:

> A - Local names, which describe a person by his place of residence or origin.
>
> B - Occupational names, which describe a person by his trade or profession.
>
> C - Surnames of relationship, which refer to the Christian name of the father or other important relative.
>
> D - Nicknames or sobriquets, coined to describe a person in terms of his appearance or character.

The name Kellogg is an interesting one, with origins that are not entirely clear, as will be discussed below.

Origins and Early Examples

The surname Kellogg is not uncommon in America: Elsdon Smith in his *American Surnames* estimated that 16,462 American citizens bore the name in 1969. In Britain however it is rare, and it is not included in the standard modern source, P H Reaney's *Dictionary of British Surnames*, or in its Victorian predecessor, C W Bardsley's *Dictionary of English and Welsh Surnames*.

The Irish surname scholar Edward MacLysaght deals in his *Supplement to Irish Families* (1964) with the surname Killough, which though 'rarely found outside northern Ulster' is derived, not from the place-name Killough in County Down but the Irish form of the Scotttish surname MacKelloch, a sept of the clan MacDonald. In 1964 MacLysaght found six Killough entries in the telephone directory from the Ballymena district (County Antrim) and other references of an earlier date from north Antrim and County Derry. However, in the case of John Killogh of Drogheda, who appears in the 1659 'census' in County Louth, MacLysaght suggests an alternative source: the English surname Kellough or Kellow, from the place-name Kelloe. He suggests further that it is this English surname which has given rise to the American form Kellogg.

MacLysaght also mentions a medieval John Kellagh, who appears in the Dublin Justiciary Rolls of 1311, but suggests that this may be a scribal attempt to record the Gaelic name Ó Ceallaigh (Kelly).

G F Black in his *Surnames of Scotland* (1946) documents the surname Kellock, which he believes may possibly derive from the Aberdeenshire place-name Keiloch. The earliest reference he cites is to Robert de Kellok (?in Aberdeenshire) who received money from the Lord Chamberlain in 1343. Other early references from Scotland are as follows:

1372 Anna de Keloche, Stirling
1495 David Kellocht, witness to deed in Fife
1567 Giles Kellock, owner of land of Primrose
1581 Alexander Kellock, burgess of Dunfermline
1606 Nicholas & William Kellok, charter at Lassodie
1650 Archibald Kellok, burgess of Kirkaldie
1666 Robert Kellock, James Kellock of Maistertown

Black treats separately the Scottish surname Killock, which, he believes, derives from the place-name Killoch in Ayrshire. The variants of Killock are however similar to those of Kellock, if not identical:

1649 John Killock, witness to tack of Little Mains of Caldwell
1657 Mungo Kelloch, parish of Kilmalcome
1685 Hellin Kellock, Tinwald
1659 John Kellock, cordwainer of Sanquhar

It is apparent from the conclusions of Black and MacLysaght that the Scottish and Irish forms Killough, Kellock and Killock, with their variants, form a confused group in which it is virtually impossible to distinguish different linguistic traditions without further study of individual families and areas. It may be that all these forms derive from the same Scottish root. It also possible that any one of these variants at some stage changed to

4

Kellogg, although we have found no specific evidence of this happening.

Distribution

We now turn to Edward Mac Lysaght's theory of the derivation of Kellogg from the place-name Kello(e), via the English form Kellough.

Kello is a parish and village in County Durham, in the north east of England. The place-name is also found independently in Scotland and has given rise to a group of surnames such as Kello(e), Kellow, Keillo and Keiloh. These names would seem to be more common in Scotland than in the north east of England.

No incidence of Kello or Kellough was found in the Durham section of the *International Genealogical Index*, which is an index of baptisms and marriages compiled by members of the Church of Latter Day Saints (now superseded by *FamilySearch*). The surname Kellow is however found in other parts of England such as Devon (where the form Kellago is also found).

C Ewen in his *Guide to the Origins of British Surnames* (1938) notes a Ric Chelloc in the Pipe Roll of 1166/7 for Lynn in Norfolk, and Ewen uses this as an example of a personal Old English name in use as a by-name (meaning here a surname that is not necessarily hereditary). Unfortunately he gives no examples of the personal name to support this, and no variant of Chelloc is mentioned in the *Oxford Dictionary of English Christian Names*.

A contemporary of Ewen, Ernest Weekley, is one of very few English writers to mention the surname Kellogg. He notes the form Keylock, which he understands to be a variant of Kellogg, and he derives Kellogg itself from a Middle English form 'Cullehog', meaning a butcher or slaughterer. He compares the similar appellation 'Cullebolloc'. Weekley's works were not intended as definitive scholarly studies, and at first sight this hypothesis might seem fanciful. However an examination of some of the evidence in the form of early will indexes and parish registers provides some evidence in its support.

Many of the American Kelloggs have traced their descent to Joseph Kellogg, who emigrated to America in the mid-seventeenth century, settling finally at Hadley in Massachusetts where he died in 1707.

Joseph was baptised at Great Leighs in Essex in 1626. An examination of the *International Genealogical Index* (which has relatively scant coverage of Essex parishes) found Joseph's baptism and with it about 75 further Kellogg (or variant) entries in the following parishes: Manuden, Debden, Braintree, Panfield, Terling, Black Notley, Mistley and Fairsted. Most of these parishes are adjacent or close to Great Leighs in north-central Essex, the exceptions being Manuden and Debden in the north-west and Mistley in the north east. Debden was the home of a family using the form Kellhogg in the sixteenth century. The earliest entries dated from the sixteenth century and none was later than the eighteenth century. Interestingly, the variants included Kellog, Kelluge, Kilhogg (1620), Kellhog(g) (16th century) and Kelhog (1720). These last three forms lend some weight to the 'slaughterer of hogs' theory. It might also be added that this part of Essex is renowned for its pig-farming.

Further parish register entries in Essex were found in the *IGI* in the same areas for the name Kellock, and some of these were clearly interchanging: one entry was for Hester Kellocke or Kellog (1660). However, no instances of Kellock were found in Essex from the sixteenth century.

A search of the *IGI* for surrounding counties found two late entries for Kent (Kelugg, Killugg); six seventeenth-century entries for Hertfordshire (Killog(g), Kellug(g)); eight seventeenth- to early eighteenth-century entries for London (Killug, Kilhog); and none for Suffolk. As a random check to see whether examples were found in other parts of England, the sections of the *IGI* for Lancashire and Yorkshire, the two largest industrial counties, were checked, but no entries found.

A search of various indexes to medieval documents including *London Feet of Fines* and a miscellaneous collection of deeds known as 'Moulton's Deeds' were checked for earlier references to the name without success. This suggested that the name was a localised one, rare nationwide. However the indexes to wills proved and administrations granted by the London Commissary Court, which covered a large number of London parishes, yielded the following:

> 1423   Rd. Kellock/Killog, citizen and goldsmith, St BrideFleet Street, London (no probate)
>
> 1625   Tho. Kilhog/Kellogg, Waltham Holy Cross, Essex, 1625 (admon)

These were particularly useful in demonstrating the relationship between the various forms, which were evidently interchangeable until well into the seventeenth century.

A useful guide to the distribution of surnames up until the eighteenth century is provided by the indexes to wills proved, and administrations granted, at the Prerogative Court of (the Archbishop of) Canterbury, which had superior jurisdiction over local ecclesiastical courts where wills were proved until 1858. The PCC thus provides a national index, though not a completely representative one, as testators who had their wills proved there were mostly among the wealthier members of society, and a disproportionate number of them were from London or Middlesex.

The PCC index was searched from 1583 to 1858 and the following noted:

1627	John Kellock/Kellocke of St Saviour, Southwark
1654	Susan Kelloge, widow, Lindsell, Essex
1656	John Killogge, bachelor, Mallendyne, Essex
1658	Thomas Kellocke, yeoman, Mylend, Colchester, Essex
1662	Robert Kellocke, Hermitage, Middlesex, mariner
1697	James Kellock (mariner) HMS Howe; HMS Russell
1706	David Kellock, mariner now bound out to sea of St John Wapping, Middlesex
1761	Nathaniel Kilhogg, bricklayer of Waltham Abbey, Essex
1763	George Kellock, belonging to HM Ship Grafton

1793   David Kellock, superannuated boatswain in
        the Navy
1805   Elizabeth Kellock, widow
1809   William Kellock, druggist of Modbury, Devon
1823   James Robert Kellock, Lieutenant RN of
        Plymouth Dock, Devon
1847   Adam Kellock, serjeant in 8th Battalion of HM
        Royal Artillery and Barrack Serjeant of Corfu,
        Ionian Islands

This indicated that the name was concentrated in Essex
and there was a high proportion of mariners (even
allowing for the fact that mariners' wills were generally
proved by the PCC). Two instances of the name, as
Kellock, appear in Devon at the beginning of the
nineteenth century and we have an earlier appearance of
the name in Southwark in 1627. There is only one
Kellog(g)(e) entry though, in Essex in 1654.

An index to probates for England and Wales (Principal
Probate Registry) for the period 1858 to 1966 found only
seven entries for the name:

1906   Justin Perkins Kellogg, Switzerland, died 12
        December 1905
1917   James Liddell Kellogg, USA, died 8 February
        1917
1918   Milo Gifford Kellogg, USA, died 26 September
        1901
1918   Ella Frances Kellogg-Jenkins
1941   David Palmer Kellogg, Manchester, died 23
        January 1941
1946   Leonard Adrian Kellogg, USA, died 27
        December 1939
1957   Frances Eliza Osborne Kellogg, USA, died 26
        September 1956

10

Most of these entries relate to Americans who had English estates. One person was of Switzerland and there is one British Kellogg, David Palmer Kellogg, who died in Manchester in 1941.

The 1873 *Return of Owners of Land*, sometimes known as the Modern Domesday, lists every owner of an acre or more in England and Wales, but includes no Kelloggs in Essex; nor does a modern telephone directory for Essex. The London Telephone Directory lists only one private individual named Kellogg.

The first decennial census return in England, Scotland and Wales was taken in 1801, but personal information was only recorded from 1841 onwards. From 1851, the age, occupation and birthplace is given for each member of the household, and so these records provide invaluable genealogical information. The latest return currently open to public inspection is that of 1911 and there are now national indexes to the returns from 1841 onwards, although these indexes are not wholly reliable. We made a brief search of the indexes for instances of the name Kellogg and variants:

6 June 1841
Kellock (302)

30 March 1851
Kellog (9); Kellock (343)

7 April 1861
Kellogg (3); Kellog (11); Kellock (423)

2 April 1871
Kellog (7); Kellock (362)

3 April 1881
Kellogg (3); Kellog (2); Kellock (365); Kellocke (1)

5 April 1891
Kellogg (2); Kellog (1); Kellock (449)

31 March 1901
Kellogg (4); Kellock (600)

2 April 1911
Kellogg (3); Kellog (1); Kellock (162)

Kellock was by far the most common of the variants, with the most appearances for the name occurring in Scotland.

A search of the indexes to births in England and Wales found 63 entries for the surname Kellogg (etc) between 1837 and 2005; there were 49 entries in the marriage indexes and 16 appearances in the death indexes for the same period.

Collections of indexes to passengers leaving the UK between 1890 and 1960 show 745 entries for the name Kellogg, most of them relating to passengers bound for the USA (there may of course be numerous duplicates). In the same period, there were 630 Kellogg arrivals in the UK, again mostly from the USA.

Printed Genealogies

The journal *New England Register* contains three genealogies for the name Kellogg:

> Kellogg, *New England Register*, vol xii, p199; vol xiv p125; vol xlviii p59

The *Concise Dictionary of American Biography* lists the following entries for people named Kellogg:

> Albert Kellogg, physician, botanist
> Clara Louise Kellogg, dramatic soprano
> Edward Kellogg, businessman, financial reformer
> Elijah Kellogg, Congregational clergyman and author
> Frank Billings Kellogg, lawyer
> Martin Kellogg, Congregational clergyman
> Samuel Henry Kellogg, Presbyterian clergyman and
>   Missionary
> William Pitt Kellogg, lawyer, Union soldier and
>   Carpet-bag politician

Another American, William Keith Kellogg (1860-1951), founded Kellogg's Company in 1906 in Battle Creek, Michigan; it is now a worldwide, billion dollar business. He and his brother, John Harvey Kellogg, created the famous cornflakes that still bear their name today.

Summary

In conclusion, the evidence suggests that the name Kellogg in England was concentrated in Essex and that several families of the name were settled in the Great Leighs area there in the seventeenth century and earlier.

Among the forms with which it interchanged was Kellock, which would seem to have an independent history in Scotland and Ireland.

The name, which was rare in England as a whole, apparently became extremely scarce if not extinct from the nineteenth century, while multiplying in America.

The earliest reference found to the surname in England dates from 1423. Only a detailed study of earlier medieval records for the Great Leighs area of Essex would make it possible to conclusively support or refute the theory that the surname Kellogg originally described a slaughterer of pigs. The history of a particular surname is rarely straightforward, since so much of the development of the name was undocumented and forms were so flexible, especially in the earliest period, and Kellogg has proved no exception. It is possible that the forms found in Essex and London, 'Kilhogg' and 'Kelhog', were later developments of a different root, and Ewen's twelfth-century reference to Ric Chelloc at Lynn might provide the clue to this. If Ewen is correct in describing Chelloc as a personal name then the forms Kilhogg and Kellhogg might have evolved as nicknames or misunderstandings of the original form.

The Irish and Scottish forms must also be taken into account in the case of American instances of the surname. Many Gaelic surnames suffered minor changes on arriving in the United States and it is certainly possible that a Scottish Killock or Keiloch became a Kellogg on the other side of the Atlantic; particularly if the surname was already known there.

On balance however it may be tentatively concluded that the evidence from parish register and probate sources supports the theory that the English name Kellogg, which was taken to America in the seventeenth century by Joseph Kellogg of Great Leighs, is an occupational surname which developed in Essex.

Sources Consulted

P H Reaney, *The Origins of English Surnames* (London: Routledge & Kegan Paul, 1967)

P H Reaney & R M Wilson, *A Dictionary of British Surnames* (Oxford: Oxford University Press, 3rd edition, 1995)

P H Reaney, *Dictionary of British Surnames* (London: Routledge & Kegan Paul, 2nd edition, 1976)

P Hanks & F Hodges, *A Dictionary of Surnames* (Oxford University Press, 1988)

M A Lower, *Patronymica Brittanica* (London, 1860)

C W Bardsley, *Dictionary of English and Welsh Surnames* (1901: reprinted, Baltimore: Genealogical Publishing Co, 1967)

C L'Estrange Ewen, *Guide to the Origin of British Surnames* (London: John Gifford, 1938)

H B Guppy, *Homes of Family Names in Great Britain* (London, 1890)

Ernest Weekley, *The Romance of Names* (London: John Murray, 2nd edition, 1917)

Ernest Weekley, *Surnames* (London: John Murray, 1917)

George F Black, *The Surnames of Scotland* (New York Public Library, 1946)

Edward MacLysaght, *The Surnames of Ireland* (Dublin: Irish University Press, 1977)

Edward MacLysaght, *Supplement to Irish Families* (Dublin: Helicon Ltd, 1964)

T J & Prys Morgan, *Welsh Surnames* (Cardiff: University of Wales Press, 1985)

F K & S Hitching, *References to English Surnames in 1601* (Walton on Thames: Bernau, 1910)

F K & S Hitching, *References to English Surnames in 1602* (Walton on Thames: Bernau, 1911)

Debrett's People of Today (Debrett's Peerage Limited: London, 1996)

The Oxford Dictionary of National Biography (online, 2004–2014)

The Concise Dictionary of National Biography, Part II, 1901–1950, (Oxford, 1961)

Burke's Family Index (London: Burke's Peerage Limited, 1976)

H R Moulton, *Palaeography, Genealogy & Topography* (Sale Catalogue, 1930)

Index to Prerogative Court of Canterbury Wills (The National Archives: online)

G W Marshall, *The Genealogist's Guide* (1903; reprinted, Baltimore: GPC 1973)

J B Whitmore, *A Genealogical Guide* (London, 1953)

Charles Bridge, *An Index to Pedigrees* (London, 1867)

Geoffrey B Barrow, *The Genealogist's Guide* (London: Research Publishing Co, 1977)

Sir Bernard Burke, *The General Armory* (London, 1884)

C R Humphrey-Smith, editor, *Burke's General Armory Volume II,* (Tabard Press, 1973)

The Return of Owners of Land (1873)

Eilert Ekwall, *The Concise Oxford Dictionary of English Place-Names* (Oxford: Clarendon Press, 4th edition, 1960)

E G Withycombe, *The Oxford Dictionary of English Christian Names* (Oxford: Clarendon Press, 2nd edition, 1950)

W J Hardy & W Page, *A Calendar to the Feet of Fines for London and Middlesex: Vol 1 Richard I – Richard III (1189–1485)* (London, 1892)

Richard McKinley, *The Surnames of Oxfordshire* (English Surnames Series III: Leopard's Head Press, 1977)

Richard McKinley, *The Surnames of Sussex* (English Surnames Series V: Leopard's Head Press, 1988)

Richard McKinley, *The Surnames of Lancashire* (English Surnames Series IV: Leopard's Head Press, 1981)

Richard McKinley, *Norfolk and Suffolk Surnames in the Middle Ages* (English Surnames Series II: Phillimore, 1975)

George Redmonds, *Yorkshire West Riding* (English Surnames Series I: Phillimore, 1973)

Mr Avenell, *The Norman People*, (London 1874)

Debrett's Heraldry (London, 1933)

J P Brooke-Little, revised, *Boutell's Heraldry* (Frederick Warne: London, 1970)

Indexes to 1841–1911 Census Returns of England and Wales (The National Archives/*Ancestry.com*)

ScotlandsPeople: Indexes to Old Parish Registers, Testaments, Statutory Registers

Concise Dictionary of American Biography (New York, 1964)

Indexes to Births, Marriages and Deaths in England and Wales 1837-2006 (Ancestry.co.uk)

National Probate Calendar for England and Wales (Principal Probate Registry) 1858-1966

UK, Outward Passenger Lists 1890-1960 (*Ancestry.co.uk*)

UK, Incoming Passenger Lists 1878-1960 (*Ancestry.co.uk*)